# Marigold's Wings

Vlasta van Kampen

GARETH**STEVENS**

PUBLISHING

A Member of the WRC Media Family of Companies

As Monarch continued the story, Marigold let her imagination run wild. She pictured herself as a butterfly, soaring high in the sky on big, wonderful wings.

Marigold was enjoying her perfect daydream when, all of a sudden, the leaf she was munching bent beneath her. With a soft *plonk*, Marigold hit the ground. For a moment, the world spun around her. Then, everything went black.

5

When Marigold opened her eyes, she was hanging upside down from a branch, just like a possum, and her skin felt funny. Remembering Monarch's story, she twisted her neck around to look at her back. Her skin had split open! Marigold wiggled and squirmed and wiggled and squirmed until her skin finally came off and fell to the ground.

A beautiful, jewel-like case now covered Marigold's body, and she knew that this magnificent covering would be her house for the next little while.

"Amazing," whispered a grasshopper.

"Incredible," said a cicada.

"How did she do that?" asked a ladybug.

For a day or two, it was very quiet both inside and outside Marigold's house. Her insect friends waited and waited, hoping she would come out. They waited until they were too curious to wait any longer.

KNOCK, KNOCK, KNOCK!

"Who is it?" said a sleepy sounding Marigold.

"What are you doing in there?" asked a bumble bee.

"Getting wings," said Marigold, now sounding more awake. "I think I'm becoming a butterfly!"

"Oh!" said the bee. "And when will you be finished?"

"Soon," said Marigold.

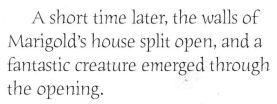

A short time later, the walls of Marigold's house split open, and a fantastic creature emerged through the opening.

"Come! Hurry! See what's happening!" shouted the grasshopper.

"Who are you?" asked an ant. "And where is Marigold?"

"It's a trick!" cried a boll weevil.

The creature stretched, slowly and carefully opening its delicate wings to the warm light of the sun. Then it moved toward a nearby milkweed.

"This is so exciting!" said the creature, in a voice that sounded just like Marigold's. "It has finally happened – just like Monarch said it would. I'm not a caterpillar anymore. I'm a butterfly. And I finally have real wings!"

All the insects stared in awe at the butterfly.

"What will you do now?" asked a curious beetle.

Marigold thought about Monarch's story.

"I think I'll fly to Mexico," she said.

"Mexico!" they all gasped. "But that's so far away."

"You're too fragile," said the bee. "You'll never make it that far."

"With these wings I will," said Marigold, who seemed very sure of herself.

"You c-ca-can't go," stammered a dragonfly. "It's much too dangerous!"

"I know," said Marigold. "But I have to go – although I'm not sure I know why."

The dragonfly looked concerned. "Even with her wings," he whispered to the bee, "Marigold will need looking after."

The bee nodded in agreement.

"I'll pass along the message," he said.

Marigold did not start her journey to Mexico right away. She spent the summer tasting flowers and testing her wings. Fluttering from petal to petal, she dreamed about her trip, and in her dreams, she saw a magical, sparkling tree. With or without wings, Marigold was still a dreamer.

One day, while Marigold was eating milkweed and daydreaming about Mexico, something scary lunged at her. Marigold beat her wings frantically and managed to escape, but as she flew high in the sky to safety, she was trembling with fear. When Marigold realized how close she had come to being eaten by a praying mantis, she thought, "I will have to pay more attention."

15

A few days later, as she was busily
flying from flower to flower, Marigold
flew right into a spider's web. She would
have ended up as the spider's dinner if a
group of dragonflies had not rushed in to
attract the spider's attention. They dive-
bombed the spider and hovered over
the web until Marigold wriggled free.

"Thank you," she called to them.
"And I promise to be more careful."

18

One mid-September morning, Marigold awoke, shivering with cold. As she looked around, she saw that the green grass of summer had turned brown. Big orange pumpkins dotted the fields, and a hint of frost covered her favorite flowers. Remembering Monarch's story, Marigold knew that the time had come to begin her long journey.

"Goodbye," she called to her friends, as she soared higher and higher above them.

Far below, the other insects waved to her and wished her a safe trip.

Flying, soaring, and gliding, Marigold fluttered southward. But when she saw the shimmering waters of the Great Lakes below her, she stopped.

"What a lot of water to cross," she thought.

Looking around, Marigold saw other monarchs roosting in nearby trees. Huddled together to keep warm, they were waiting until morning to cross the lakes. Marigold decided to wait with them.

The next morning , the monarchs awoke and stretched their wings. The day was warm, but the trees were tipped with orange. Marigold's instincts told her there was no time to lose. Off flew the monarchs – some together, some alone – looking for air currents to help carry them across the cold waters of the Great Lakes.

On the other side of the lakes, Marigold stopped to rest on a blade of grass. She was exhausted — too tired even to notice a cow munching grass nearby. The cow did not see Marigold, either, but just as she chomped down on the grass where Marigold was resting, a swarm of bees rushed in and buzzed around the cow's nose and ears. The cow shook her head and dropped her mouthful of grass.

"Thank you, bees." cried Marigold as she flew to safety. "What a fright that was!"

"We were happy to help," said the bees, "but please try to be more careful."

The bees flew off, shaking their fuzzy heads. "She'll never make it," they muttered.

The days and weeks passed, and Marigold flew onward, always heading south. Because one of her wings was damaged during the journey, she needed to rest more often now. Spotting a pond below, she gently fluttered down onto a lily pad. An enormous toad watched her land and quickly flicked out his long tongue to capture her for his dinner. Using her last burst of energy, Marigold flitted beyond the toad's reach. An air current picked her up.

As the wind carried her on toward Mexico, Marigold whispered, "I can't go any further. My wings are tired and broken. I need to stop." She had been traveling for two months.

Just then, Marigold felt a strange quivering in the tips of her antennae. The quivering worked its way through her whole body to the edges of her wings, and Marigold knew that she had reached her destination. She was in the mountains of Mexico — at last!

Looking at her new surroundings, Marigold realized she was not alone. Millions of other monarchs fluttered alongside her, and a mariachi band was there to welcome them. It was a fiesta!

Then, suddenly, Marigold saw the tree. It was just as she had imagined – magical and sparkling, thanks to the jeweled decorations that covered its branches. When Marigold looked closely, she realized that the sparkling decorations were not decorations at all. They were millions of monarchs, all clinging to the tree's branches. Marigold swooped down onto the tree, as she knew she should. Her journey was complete.

Marigold lay still on the ground. All of her insect friends were around her. Slowly, she opened one eye, then the other.

"She's not dead!" they cried.

"I certainly am not," said Marigold, scrambling to her feet, "but what a dream I had!"

Just as Marigold started to tell her friends about her dream, she felt a strange quivering in the tips of her antennae.

"It's happening!" Marigold cried, jumping up and down with excitement. "It's not a dream this time. I'm finally going to become a butterfly with big, wonderful wings! It's really and truly going to happen!"

And it really and truly did.

# More about Marigold's Journey

Monarch butterflies really do fly to Mexico, and they meet up with different insects and other animals along the way. Monarch butterflies make the most amazing and wonderful journey in the insect kingdom. Many fly all the way to Mexico from Canada and the northeastern United States. At a distance of almost 3,000 miles (4,800 kilometers), that's a very long trip! For people to make a similar journey, relative to size, they would have to walk all the way around the world at least once.

What's even more amazing about monarchs' journeys is that up to five generations can pass between trips. Imagine traveling to a place your great-great-grandparents had been, without asking anyone for directions. How would you know where to go? How do the monarchs find their way? No one really knows.

The real journey to Mexico is far more dangerous than the one in Marigold's dream. As they travel, monarchs must deal with rain, wind, and storms of all kinds. They must fly across lakes, rivers, mountains, and other natural barriers. And, everywhere they go, there are people. People are the source of dangers such as pollution, pesticides, and highways. Sadly, cars and trucks probably kill more monarch butterflies than weather, natural barriers, and all the animals Marigold meets on her journey.

Given the danger, the length, and the difficulty of the journey, the real wonder is not that Marigold dreams of flying to Mexico, but that she actually makes it all the way there and lives to have caterpillars of her own.

— DR. PHIL SCHAPPERT